TOFU

COOKBOOK FOR BEGINNERS

Copyright © 2023.

All rights reserved.
No part of this book may be reproduced in any form
or by any electronic or mechanical means,
including information storage and retrieval systems,
without written permission from the author,
except for the use of brief quotations in a book review

Table of Contents

Tofu Curry 5

Teriyaki Tofu... 7

Tofu Omelette 9

Crispy Tofu And Dipping Sauce 11

Tofu Salad 13

Vegan BBQ Tofu 15

Vegan Smoked Tofu Burger 17

Mapo Tofu 19

Steamed White Tofu 21

Pad Thai 23

Stir-Fried Basil with Minced Pork and Tofu 25

Stir-Fried Tofu 27

Cabbage Clear Soup with Tofu and Minced Pork 29

Fried Tofu with Ginger 31

Tofu French Fries 33

Avocado Tofu Salad 35

Stir-Fried Bean Sprouts with Tofu 37

Steamed Stuffed Tofu with Soy Sauce 39

Tofu Fried Rice 41

Soft Tofu Kimchi Soup 43

Roasted Tofu With Chili And Salt 45

Green Curry With Tofu 47

Fried Tofu With Tamarind Sauce 49

Tofu And Pork Hamburger 51

Spinach Tofu Cutlets 53

Tofu Steamed Egg 55

Tofu Tomato Sauce Pasta 57

Baked Tofu With Vermicelli 59

Spinach Pesto With Tofu 61

Tofu Meatballs 63

Tofu Curry

Tofu Curry is a delicious and satisfying vegetarian dish that combines the soft, silky texture of tofu with rich, complex curry flavors. This dish is a popular staple in many Asian and Indian cuisines and can be customized with various vegetables and spices to suit individual tastes. So whether you're a vegetarian or simply looking to add more plant-based meals to your diet, Tofu Curry is an excellent choice for a healthy and satisfying meal that is easy to prepare and packed with flavor.

Ingredients:

- 1 block of firm tofu, pressed and cut into small cubes
- 1 tablespoon vegetable oil
- 1 onion, chopped
- 3 garlic cloves, minced
- 1 tablespoon ginger, minced
- 1 tablespoon curry powder
- 1 teaspoon cumin
- 1 teaspoon coriander
- 1 teaspoon turmeric
- 1/4 teaspoon cayenne pepper (optional)
- 1 can (14 oz) coconut milk
- 1 cup vegetable broth
- 1 tablespoon soy sauce
- 1 tablespoon brown sugar

- 2 cups mixed vegetables (such as bell peppers, zucchini, and carrots)
- Salt and pepper to taste
- Fresh cilantro for garnish (optional)

Instructions:

1. In a large skillet, heat the oil over medium-high heat. Add the tofu cubes and cook until golden brown, occasionally stirring, for about 5 minutes. Remove the tofu from the skillet and set aside.
2. Add the onion, garlic, and ginger in the same skillet, and cook for 2-3 minutes until the onion is soft and translucent.
3. Add the curry powder, cumin, coriander, turmeric, and cayenne pepper (if using) to the skillet and cook for 1 minute, until fragrant.
4. Pour the coconut milk, vegetable broth, soy sauce, and brown sugar, and stir to combine. Bring the mixture to a boil, then reduce the heat to low and let it simmer for 10-15 minutes until the sauce has thickened slightly.
5. Add the mixed vegetables to the skillet and stir to combine. Cook for 5-7 minutes, until the vegetables are tender.
6. Add the cooked tofu back to the skillet and stir to combine—season with salt and pepper to taste.
7. Serve the tofu curry over rice or noodles and garnish with fresh cilantro, if desired.

Teriyaki Tofu

This Teriyaki Tofu recipe is a delicious and healthy way to enjoy Japanese cuisine's savory and sweet flavors. The formula features cubes of firm tofu marinated in a homemade teriyaki sauce, then quickly sautéed to create a mouth-watering and protein-packed dish. The rich and flavorful teriyaki sauce is made with a combination of soy sauce, mirin, ginger, garlic, and brown sugar and can be customized to individual tastes. This recipe is quick and easy to make and can be served with various vegetables, grains, or noodles for a satisfying and delicious meal that is perfect for lunch or dinner.

Ingredients:

- 1 block of firm tofu, pressed and cut into small cubes
- 1 tablespoon vegetable oil
- 2 tablespoons cornstarch
- Salt and pepper to taste
- 1/2 cup soy sauce
- 1/4 cup honey
- 1/4 cup rice vinegar
- 2 garlic cloves, minced
- 1 tablespoon ginger, minced
- 2 tablespoons water
- 1 tablespoon sesame seeds
- Sliced green onions for garnish (optional)

Instructions:

1. To make the teriyaki sauce, mix the soy sauce, honey, rice vinegar, garlic, ginger, and water in a medium bowl. Set aside.
2. In a large bowl, toss the cubed tofu with cornstarch, salt, and pepper until evenly coated.
3. In a large skillet, heat the oil over medium-high heat. Add the tofu cubes and cook until golden brown, occasionally stirring, for about 5 minutes.
4. Pour the teriyaki sauce over the tofu in the skillet and stir to combine. Bring the mixture to a simmer and cook for 2-3 minutes, until the sauce has thickened and the tofu is fully coated.
5. Sprinkle sesame seeds over the tofu and stir to combine.
6. If desired, serve the teriyaki tofu over rice and garnish with sliced green onions.

Tofu Omelette

Tofu omelets are a delicious, healthy, and versatile breakfast dish that can be enjoyed by vegetarians and meat-eaters alike. Tofu omelets are the perfect option if you're looking for an easy egg-free meal to make in the morning. Packed with protein and nutrients, this vegan version of an omelet is sure to keep you full until lunchtime.

Ingredients:

- 1 block of firm tofu, pressed and crumbled
- 1 tablespoon vegetable oil
- 1/2 cup diced onion
- 1/2 cup chopped bell pepper
- 2 garlic cloves, minced
- 1 teaspoon turmeric
- 1 teaspoon nutritional yeast (optional)
- Salt and pepper to taste
- Sliced green onions for garnish (optional)

Instructions:

1. In a large skillet, heat the oil over medium-high heat. Add the onion, bell pepper, and garlic, and cook for 2-3 minutes, until the onion is soft and translucent.
2. Add the crumbled tofu to the skillet and stir to combine with the vegetables.
3. Sprinkle turmeric and nutritional yeast (if using) over the tofu mixture and stir to combine—season with salt and pepper to taste.

4. Cook the tofu mixture for 5-7 minutes, occasionally stirring until the tofu is heated through and has taken on the yellow color of the turmeric.
5. Use a spatula to fold the tofu omelet in half, and cook for another 1-2 minutes to set the shape.
6. Slide the tofu omelet onto a plate, and garnish with sliced green onions, if desired.

Crispy Tofu And Dipping Sauce

Tofu is a popular, versatile, and nutritious food that can be prepared in many different ways. This recipe will provide an easy and delicious recipe for Crispy Tofu. Perfectly seasoned and pan-fried, it's the perfect addition to any meal, whether as a side dish or main course. Not only is this recipe delicious, but it can also be vegan-friendly and gluten-free with the right ingredients.

Crispy Tofu
Ingredients:

- 1 block of firm tofu, pressed and cut into bite-size pieces
- 1/4 cup cornstarch
- 1/4 teaspoon garlic powder
- 1/4 teaspoon onion powder
- 1/4 teaspoon paprika
- Salt and pepper to taste
- 2 tablespoons vegetable oil

Instructions:

1. Mix the cornstarch, garlic powder, onion powder, paprika, salt, and pepper in a shallow dish.
2. Add the tofu pieces to the cornstarch mixture and gently toss to coat evenly.
3. In a large skillet, heat the oil over medium-high heat.
4. Once the oil is hot, add the tofu pieces to the skillet in a single layer, making sure not to overcrowd the skillet.

Cook for 2-3 minutes on each side until golden brown and crispy.
5. Use a slotted spoon to transfer the crispy tofu to a plate lined with paper towels, to remove any excess oil.
6. Serve the crispy tofu as is or as a topping for salads, rice bowls, or stir-fries.

Dipping Sauce
Ingredients:
- 160 grams of sugar
- 80 grams of vinegar
- 1 1/2 teaspoons salt
- 3-5 red peppers/chili peppers
- 2 cilantro
- 3 tbsp roasted peanuts

Instructions:
1. Mix sugar with vinegar and salt and bring the ingredients to a simmer. Use medium light.
2. Stir until all ingredients are well dissolved. When it boils, turn off the heat to low heat. Continue to simmer for a while until the smell of vinegar fades. Then, please turn off the stove and take it out to cool down.
3. When the stewed sauce is cool. (Notice that it will look thicker and more sticky)
4. Grind the peanuts until coarse.
5. Scoop the sauce into a cup. Sprinkle peanuts as desired, followed by chili and coriander. Ready to serve.

Tofu Salad

Tofu Salad is a delicious, healthy, vegan-friendly salad that can be enjoyed as a main meal or side dish. It is a perfect option for adding more plant-based proteins to their diet. Made with firm tofu, this salad is packed with protein, minerals, and vitamins essential for our bodies. Combining the right ingredients gives it a unique flavor, making it enjoyable.

Ingredients:

- 1 block of firm tofu, pressed and cut into bite-size pieces
- 6 cups mixed greens
- 1 cucumber, sliced
- 1 red bell pepper, sliced
- 1 carrot, shredded
- 1/4 cup sliced red onion
- 1/4 cup chopped fresh cilantro
- 1/4 cup chopped peanuts
- For the dressing:
- 1/4 cup rice vinegar
- 1 tablespoon soy sauce
- 1 tablespoon honey
- 1 tablespoon sesame oil
- 1 tablespoon grated ginger
- 1 garlic clove, minced

Instructions:

1. Whisk together the rice vinegar, soy sauce, honey, sesame oil, grated ginger, and minced garlic in a small bowl to make the dressing. Set aside.
2. In a large bowl, combine the mixed greens, sliced cucumber, bell pepper, shredded carrot, and red onion.
3. In a large skillet, heat a tablespoon of oil over medium-high heat. Add the tofu pieces and cook for 5-7 minutes, occasionally stirring, until they are golden brown and crispy.
4. Add the crispy tofu to the salad, and toss to combine.
5. Drizzle the dressing over the salad, and toss to coat evenly.
6. Garnish the salad with chopped cilantro and chopped peanuts.
7. Serve the tofu salad immediately, and enjoy!
8. This recipe is customizable, so feel free to add or substitute any of the veggies, herbs, or nuts to your preference.

Vegan BBQ Tofu

Vegan BBQ Tofu is a delicious and nutritious way to enjoy the flavors of summer grilling without the use of animal products. If you're looking for a vegan version of traditional barbecue, this vegan BBQ Tofu will hit the spot! It's simple to prepare, full of flavor, and ready in just thirty minutes.

Ingredients:

- 1 block of firm tofu, pressed and cut into 1/2-inch slices
- 1/2 cup BBQ sauce
- 2 tablespoons soy sauce
- 1 tablespoon olive oil
- 1 tablespoon apple cider vinegar
- 1 teaspoon smoked paprika
- 1/2 teaspoon garlic powder
- Salt and pepper to taste

Instructions:

1. Preheat the oven to 400°F (200°C).
2. In a small bowl, whisk together the BBQ sauce, soy sauce, olive oil, apple cider vinegar, smoked paprika, garlic powder, salt, and pepper to make the marinade.
3. Place the tofu slices in a shallow dish, and pour the marinade over them. Use a pastry brush or your hands to coat the tofu evenly with the marinade.
4. Let the tofu marinate in the refrigerator for at least 30 minutes or up to 24 hours.

5. Once the tofu is marinated, transfer the tofu and the marinade to a baking sheet lined with parchment paper. Bake for 20-25 minutes, flipping the tofu halfway through until the tofu is crispy and caramelized.
6. Serve the BBQ tofu hot with your favorite side dishes such as coleslaw, grilled veggies, or corn on the cob.

Vegan Smoked Tofu Burger

Vegan cuisine has become increasingly popular recently, with even the most dedicated meat-eaters succumbing to its deliciousness. So if you're looking for a delicious vegan burger option, look no further than the vegan smoked tofu burger. This burger is vegan, full of flavor, and surprisingly easy to make. The tofu's smoky flavor combined with various ingredients gives this burger an unforgettable taste that will have you hooked after just one bite.

Ingredients:

- 1 block of smoked tofu, sliced into patties
- 4 whole wheat burger buns
- 4 lettuce leaves
- 4 slices of tomato
- 1/2 red onion, sliced
- For the sauce:
- 1/4 cup vegan mayonnaise
- 1 tablespoon Dijon mustard
- 1 teaspoon smoked paprika
- Salt and pepper to taste

Instructions:

1. Whisk together the vegan mayonnaise, dijon mustard, smoked paprika, salt, and pepper in a small bowl to make the sauce. Set aside.
2. Preheat a skillet over medium-high heat. Once the skillet is hot, add the smoked tofu patties, and cook for about

3-4 minutes on each side, until they are crispy and heated through.
3. While the tofu is cooking, toast the burger buns and prepare the toppings.
4. To assemble the burgers, spread the sauce on the bottom half of the burger buns. Next, add a lettuce leaf, a slice of tomato, and some sliced red onion.
5. Once the tofu is cooked, place a tofu patty on top of the toppings, and add more sauce on top of the tofu.
6. Top the burger with the other half of the burger bun, and serve immediately.

Mapo Tofu

Mapo Tofu, also known as Mapo Dofu, is a classic Chinese dish from the Sichuan province in China. It consists of soft tofu cubes cooked in a spicy chili and bean-based sauce. This traditional dish has made its way around the world, becoming one of the most popular dishes in Chinese cuisine. Not only is it delicious, but it's also elementary to make and can be enjoyed both hot or cold.

Ingredients:

- 1 block of firm tofu, cut into small cubes
- 2 tablespoons Sichuan peppercorns
- 1/4 cup vegetable oil
- 1 tablespoon chili bean paste (doubanjiang)
- 2 garlic cloves, minced
- 1 tablespoon grated ginger
- 1/2 cup vegetable broth
- 2 tablespoons soy sauce
- 1 tablespoon hoisin sauce
- 1 teaspoon sugar
- 1 tablespoon cornstarch mixed with 2 tablespoons water
- 2 green onions, thinly sliced

Instructions:

1. Toast the Sichuan peppercorns in a dry skillet over medium heat until fragrant, about 1-2 minutes. Grind

them into a fine powder using a mortar, pestle, or spice grinder.
2. Heat the vegetable oil in a wok or large skillet over medium-high heat. Once the oil is hot, add the chili bean paste, minced garlic, and grated ginger. Stir-fry for about 30 seconds, until fragrant.
3. Add the cubed tofu to the wok and stir-fry gently for about 2-3 minutes.
4. Pour the vegetable broth, soy sauce, hoisin sauce, and sugar. Stir to combine and bring to a boil.
5. Add the cornstarch mixture to the wok, and stir until the sauce thickens.
6. Add the ground Sichuan peppercorns to the wok and stir to combine.
7. Transfer the Mapo Tofu to a serving dish, and garnish with sliced green onions.
8. Serve hot with steamed rice.

Steamed White Tofu

Tofu is a versatile, healthy, and affordable ingredient. It has been eaten in many cultures for centuries. Steamed white tofu is an effortless dish that can easily be incorporated into any meal. Not only is it delicious, but it also packs plenty of essential nutrients making it an excellent choice for those looking to add variety to their diet while keeping health in mind.

Ingredients:

- 1 block of white tofu
- 1 tablespoon soy sauce
- 1 tablespoon sesame oil
- 1 tablespoon chopped scallions or green onions
- 1 teaspoon minced garlic
- 1 teaspoon grated ginger

Instructions:

1. Cut the tofu into thin slices, and arrange them in a single layer in a heatproof dish that fits inside a steamer basket.
2. Mix the soy sauce, sesame oil, chopped scallions, minced garlic, and grated ginger in a small bowl to make the sauce.
3. Drizzle the sauce over the tofu, and spread it evenly to coat it.

4. Fill a steamer basket with enough water to come up to the bottom of the heatproof dish. Place the plate of tofu in the steamer basket.
5. Cover the steamer basket with a lid, and steam the tofu for 10-12 minutes until it is heated.
6. Once the tofu is steamed, please remove it from the steamer basket and transfer it to a serving dish.
7. Garnish the tofu with more chopped scallions or green onions, and serve hot.

Pad Thai

Pad Thai is a popular dish in Thailand, served as street food and in restaurants across the country. It is considered one of Thai cuisine's most well-known and beloved dishes. Featuring rice noodles, chicken or shrimp, eggs, and various vegetables such as bean sprouts and garlic chives, Pad Thai can be made in different ways. It has become a staple in many cultures worldwide due to its delicious flavor and versatile ingredients.

Ingredients:

- 8 oz. dried rice noodles
- 2 tablespoons vegetable oil
- 2 garlic cloves, minced
- 1 small shallot, minced
- 1/2 pound firm tofu, cut into small pieces
- 2 large eggs, lightly beaten
- 1/4 cup chopped roasted peanuts
- 1/4 cup chopped scallions
- 1/4 cup fresh bean sprouts
- Lime wedges for serving

For the sauce:

- 2 tablespoons tamarind paste
- 2 tablespoons fish sauce or vegan fish sauce alternative
- 1 tablespoon palm sugar or brown sugar
- 1 tablespoon soy sauce
- 1/2 teaspoon paprika

- 1/2 teaspoon chili flakes

Instructions:

1. Soak the rice noodles in warm water for 30 minutes or until they are soft and pliable.
2. In a small bowl, whisk together the tamarind paste, fish sauce, palm sugar, soy sauce, paprika, and chili flakes to make the sauce. Set aside.
3. Heat the vegetable oil in a wok or large skillet over medium-high heat. Add garlic, shallot, and stir-fry for about 30 seconds until fragrant.
4. Add the tofu to the wok, and stir-fry for about 2-3 minutes, until it is lightly browned.
5. Push the tofu to the side of the wok, and pour the beaten eggs into the other side. Scramble the eggs until they are set, then mix them with the tofu.
6. Drain the soaked rice noodles, and add them to the wok. Stir-fry for about 2-3 minutes, until the noodles are soft and coated with the sauce.
7. Add the chopped roasted peanuts, chopped scallions, and fresh bean sprouts to the wok, and stir-fry for another 1-2 minutes, until the vegetables are slightly wilted.
8. Transfer the Pad Thai to a serving dish, and garnish with more chopped peanuts and scallions.
9. Serve hot with lime wedges on the side.

Stir-Fried Basil with Minced Pork and Tofu

Stir-fried basil with minced pork and tofu is a classic Thai dish with a powerful punch of flavor. With just a few simple ingredients, this delicious dish can be on the dinner table in no time. It combines fragrant Thai basil with savory minced pork and tofu for a unique blend of textures and tastes. Its bold flavors make it an ideal accompaniment to steamed jasmine rice or noodles, making it a complete meal that will satisfy any appetite.

Ingredients:

- 1/2 pound minced pork
- 1/2 block firm tofu, cut into small pieces
- 2 tablespoons vegetable oil
- 3 garlic cloves, minced
- 2 Thai chilies, minced (or substitute with chili flakes to taste)
- 1/2 cup fresh basil leaves, loosely packed
- 1 tablespoon fish sauce or vegan fish sauce alternative
- 1 tablespoon soy sauce
- 1 teaspoon oyster sauce or vegan oyster sauce alternative
- 1/2 teaspoon palm sugar or brown sugar
- Steamed rice for serving

Instructions:

1. Heat the vegetable oil in a wok or large skillet over medium-high heat. Add the minced garlic and Thai chilies, and stir-fry for about 30 seconds until fragrant.
2. Add the minced pork to the wok, and stir-fry for about 2-3 minutes until it is browned and cooked.
3. Add the firm tofu to the wok and stir-fry for another 1-2 minutes until it is heated.
4. In a small bowl, whisk together the fish sauce, soy sauce, oyster sauce, and palm sugar to make the sauce.
5. Pour the sauce over the pork and tofu in the wok, and stir-fry for another 1-2 minutes until the ingredients are well coated with the sauce.
6. Add the fresh basil leaves to the wok, and stir-fry for another 30 seconds until the basil leaves are wilted and fragrant.
7. Transfer the stir-fry to a serving dish, and serve hot with steamed rice on the side.

Stir-Fried Tofu

Stir-fried tofu is a delicious and healthy alternative to traditional fried food. It's also an easy meal for anyone to make. So whether you're vegan, vegetarian, or just trying to eat healthier, stir-fried tofu is a great dish to add to your repertoire of recipes. This recipe will provide step-by-step instructions on how to make this fantastic dish.

Ingredients:

- 1 block firm tofu, drained and cut into small pieces
- 2 tablespoons vegetable oil
- 2 garlic cloves, minced
- 1 red bell pepper, sliced
- 1 green bell pepper, sliced
- 1 onion, sliced
- 1 tablespoon soy sauce
- 1 tablespoon oyster sauce or vegan oyster sauce alternative
- Salt and pepper, to taste
- Green onions, chopped, for garnish

Instructions:

1. Heat the vegetable oil in a wok or large skillet over medium-high heat. Add the minced garlic, and stir-fry for about 30 seconds, until fragrant.

2. Add the sliced red and green bell peppers and onion to the wok, and stir-fry for about 3-4 minutes, until the vegetables are slightly softened.
3. Add the firm tofu to the wok, and stir-fry for another 2-3 minutes, until the tofu is lightly browned on all sides.
4. In a small bowl, whisk together the soy sauce and oyster sauce to make the sauce.
5. Pour the sauce over the tofu and vegetables in the wok, and stir-fry for another 1-2 minutes, until the ingredients are well coated with the sauce.
6. Season with salt and pepper to taste.
7. Transfer the stir-fry to a serving dish, and garnish with chopped green onions.
8. Serve hot with steamed rice or as a side dish.

Cabbage Clear Soup with Tofu and Minced Pork

Cabbage Clear Soup with Tofu and Minced Pork is an easy yet flavorful meal that comes together quickly with minimal effort. This traditional Chinese recipe makes a great lunch or dinner option and is surprisingly healthy. Combining tofu, pork, and cabbage creates a unique flavor profile that everyone can enjoy. The broth for this soup is light, but it's packed with lots of flavors from the vegetables, herbs, and spices used in the recipe.

Ingredients:

- 1/2 pound minced pork
- 1/2 block firm tofu, cut into small cubes
- 1/2 head cabbage, chopped
- 6 cups water or vegetable broth
- 2 tablespoons vegetable oil
- 3 garlic cloves, minced
- 1 teaspoon grated ginger
- 2 tablespoons soy sauce
- Salt and pepper, to taste
- Chopped scallions for garnish

Instructions:

1. Heat the vegetable oil in a large pot over medium-high heat. Add the minced garlic and grated ginger, and stir-fry for about 30 seconds until fragrant.

2. Add the minced pork to the pot, and stir-fry for about 2-3 minutes until it is browned and cooked.
3. Add the chopped cabbage to the pot and stir-fry for another 2-3 minutes until the cabbage is slightly softened.
4. Pour in the water or vegetable broth, and bring to a boil.
5. Add the cubed tofu and soy sauce to the pot, and let the soup simmer for about 10-15 minutes until the vegetables are cooked through, and the flavors are well blended.
6. Season with salt and pepper to taste.
7. Serve hot in individual bowls, and garnish with chopped scallions.

Fried Tofu with Ginger

Fried tofu with ginger is an incredibly flavorful and healthy vegan dish that's easy to make. It's an ideal meal for those looking to cut down on their meat intake, as the tofu packs a protein punch without any saturated fat often found in animal products. In addition, the combination of fried tofu and ginger makes for a delicious balance of sweet and savory flavors.

Ingredients:

- 1 block of firm tofu, cut into bite-sized pieces
- 1 tablespoon cornstarch
- 1 tablespoon vegetable oil
- 2 tablespoons grated ginger
- 2 garlic cloves, minced
- 1 tablespoon soy sauce
- 1 tablespoon oyster sauce or vegan oyster sauce alternative
- 1 tablespoon rice vinegar
- 1 teaspoon sugar
- 2 green onions, sliced
- Salt and pepper, to taste

Instructions:

1. Toss the bite-sized tofu pieces with cornstarch to coat them lightly.
2. Heat the vegetable oil in a large non-stick skillet over medium-high heat. Add the coated tofu pieces to the

skillet, and cook for about 2-3 minutes on each side until the tofu is lightly browned and crispy. Transfer the tofu to a plate.
3. Add the grated ginger and minced garlic in the same skillet, and stir-fry for about 30 seconds, until fragrant.
4. In a small bowl, whisk together the soy sauce, oyster sauce, rice vinegar, and sugar to make the sauce.
5. Pour the sauce into the skillet with the ginger and garlic, and stir to combine.
6. Return the crispy tofu pieces to the skillet, and stir-fry for another 1-2 minutes, until the tofu is coated with the sauce and heated through.
7. Season with salt and pepper to taste.
8. Serve hot, garnished with sliced green onions.

Tofu French Fries

Tofu French fries may sound strange, but they are a delicious and healthy alternative to traditional french fries. Making tofu fries is surprisingly easy and can be served as an appetizer or side dish. These delicious vegan-friendly fries are packed with protein and provide a crunchy texture perfect for dipping in ketchup or your favorite sauce.

Ingredients:

- 1 extra block of firm tofu
- 1/4 cup cornstarch
- 1/4 cup all-purpose flour
- 1 teaspoon garlic powder
- 1 teaspoon onion powder
- 1/2 teaspoon paprika
- 1/4 teaspoon salt
- 1/4 teaspoon black pepper
- Vegetable oil for frying

Instructions:

1. Drain and press the tofu to remove excess water. Cut the tofu into thin sticks about the size of french fries.
2. Mix the cornstarch, all-purpose flour, garlic powder, onion powder, paprika, salt, and black pepper in a shallow dish.
3. Roll the tofu sticks in the flour mixture, ensuring they are well coated.

4. Heat the vegetable oil in a deep fryer or a large pot over medium-high heat to 375°F.
5. Fry the tofu sticks in the hot oil, in batches, for about 3-4 minutes until they are golden brown and crispy. Use a slotted spoon to remove the fries from the oil, and drain them on a paper towel-lined plate.
6. Serve hot with ketchup, aioli, or your favorite dipping sauce.

Avocado Tofu Salad

Avocado tofu salad is an easy and delicious dish for lunch or dinner. It is full of flavor and nutrition, making it a great way to get some essential vitamins and minerals. The combination of the creamy avocado, protein-rich tofu, and crunchy vegetables make for a satisfying meal that can be served hot or cold. Plus, this vegan-friendly dish is simple to prepare and can be customized with your favorite ingredients.

Ingredients:

- 1 block firm tofu, drained and pressed
- 2 ripe avocados, pitted and diced
- 1 small red onion, diced
- 1 red bell pepper, diced
- 1/4 cup chopped cilantro
- 1/4 cup lime juice
- 2 tablespoons olive oil
- 1 tablespoon honey or agave nectar
- Salt and pepper, to taste

Instructions:

1. Cut the drained and pressed tofu into small cubes.
2. Mix the diced avocado, red onion, red bell pepper, and chopped cilantro in a large bowl.
3. Whisk together the lime juice, olive oil, honey or agave nectar, salt, and pepper in a small bowl.
4. Add the cubed tofu to the bowl with the avocado mixture.

5. Pour the dressing over the tofu and avocado mixture, and toss gently to combine.
6. Adjust the seasoning with salt and pepper to taste.
7. Chill the salad in the refrigerator for at least 30 minutes before serving to allow the flavors to meld.
8. Serve cold, garnished with additional cilantro, if desired.

Stir-Fried Bean Sprouts with Tofu

Stir-frying is a quick and easy way to get a delicious meal on the table. Bean sprouts are an excellent addition to any stir fry, as they add crunch and freshness. Combined with tofu, bean sprouts can create a substantial meal that is both nutritious and tasty. In this recipe, we will explore the steps needed to make Stir Fried Bean Sprouts with Tofu, a dish sure to satisfy vegetarians and meat eaters alike.

Ingredients:

- 1 block of firm tofu, drained and cut into small cubes
- 2 cups bean sprouts, washed and drained
- 1 small onion, chopped
- 1 small red bell pepper, sliced
- 2 cloves garlic, minced
- 1 tablespoon soy sauce
- 1 teaspoon oyster sauce (optional)
- 1 teaspoon sesame oil
- Salt and pepper, to taste
- Vegetable oil for frying

Instructions:

1. Heat a tablespoon of vegetable oil in a wok or large skillet over medium-high heat.
2. Add the cubed tofu and stir-fry for 2-3 minutes, until lightly browned. Remove the tofu from the wok and set aside.

3. Add another tablespoon of oil to the wok, and add the chopped onion and sliced red bell pepper. Stir-fry for 1-2 minutes, until the vegetables are slightly softened.
4. Add the minced garlic to the wok and stir-fry for another 30 seconds.
5. Add the bean sprouts to the wok, and stir-fry for 1-2 minutes until the bean sprouts are slightly wilted.
6. Add the soy sauce, oyster sauce (if using), and sesame oil to the wok and stir-fry for another minute.
7. Add the cooked tofu to the wok, and stir-fry for another 1-2 minutes, until the tofu is heated.
8. Adjust the seasoning with salt and pepper to taste.
9. Serve hot, garnished with chopped scallions or cilantro, if desired.

Steamed Stuffed Tofu with Soy Sauce

Tofu is one of the most versatile ingredients in many Asian dishes, and steamed stuffed tofu with soy sauce is no exception. This flavorful recipe is easy to make and requires minimal ingredients. This dish is perfect for a light lunch or an appetizer for a dinner party. Steamed stuffed tofu with soy sauce tastes delicious and can be easily modified to suit different dietary needs.

Ingredients:

- 1 block firm tofu, cut into 6 thick slices
- 1/2 cup ground pork
- 1/2 cup chopped shrimp
- 1/4 cup chopped water chestnuts
- 1/4 cup chopped scallions
- 1 tablespoon soy sauce
- 1 tablespoon Shaoxing wine (or dry sherry)
- 1 teaspoon sesame oil
- Salt and pepper, to taste
- 1 tablespoon cornstarch
- 1 tablespoon water
- 1/4 cup soy sauce
- 1/4 cup chicken stock or water
- 1 teaspoon sugar
- 1 teaspoon sesame oil
- 1 tablespoon cornstarch

- 2 tablespoons water

Instructions:

1. Cut the tofu into 6 thick slices, and use a spoon to hollow out a small cavity in the center of each piece. Set aside.
2. In a mixing bowl, combine the ground pork, chopped shrimp, water chestnuts, scallions, soy sauce, Shaoxing wine, sesame oil, salt, and pepper. Mix well.
3. Stuff each tofu slice with a generous amount of the pork and shrimp mixture.
4. Whisk together the cornstarch and water in a small bowl to make a slurry.
5. Place the stuffed tofu slices in a steamer basket or heatproof plate.
6. Steam the stuffed tofu over high heat for 10-15 minutes until cooked.
7. While the tofu is steaming, make the soy sauce glaze. Mix the soy sauce, chicken stock or water, sugar, and sesame oil in a small saucepan. Bring to a simmer over medium heat.
8. Whisk together the cornstarch and water in a small bowl to make a slurry. Add the cornstarch slurry to the soy sauce mixture, and whisk well to combine. Cook for 1-2 minutes, until the sauce, has thickened.
9. Transfer it to a serving plate when the stuffed tofu is cooked through.
10. Spoon the soy sauce glaze over the stuffed tofu slices.
11. Garnish with chopped scallions or cilantro, if desired.

Tofu Fried Rice

Tofu Fried Rice is an incredibly versatile and flavorful dish that can be whipped up in minutes. It's a great way to use leftover rice, making it a budget-friendly choice for any night of the week. This vegan-friendly dish is packed with protein from tofu, and adding vegetables makes it both nutritious and delicious.

Ingredients:

- 3 cups cooked rice, cooled
- 1 block of firm tofu, cut into small cubes
- 1 small onion, diced
- 1 small carrot, diced
- 1/2 cup frozen peas
- 2 cloves garlic, minced
- 2 tablespoons vegetable oil
- 2 tablespoons soy sauce
- 1 tablespoon oyster sauce (can be substituted with hoisin sauce or soy sauce)
- 1/2 teaspoon sugar
- Salt and pepper, to taste
- 2 green onions, sliced (optional)

Instructions:

1. Heat the vegetable oil over medium-high heat in a large wok or skillet.
2. Add the diced onion and sauté until it's soft and translucent about 2-3 minutes.

3. Add the diced carrot and frozen peas to the skillet and continue to sauté for 2-3 minutes.
4. Add the minced garlic to the skillet and stir for about 30 seconds until fragrant.
5. Add the cubed tofu to the skillet and cook for 2-3 minutes, occasionally stirring until the tofu is lightly browned.
6. Add the cooked rice to the skillet and mix with the vegetables and tofu.
7. Whisk together the soy sauce, oyster sauce (or hoisin sauce), sugar, salt, and pepper in a small bowl.
8. Pour the sauce mixture over the rice and stir until everything is well combined and the rice is evenly coated.
9. Cook the rice mixture for another 2-3 minutes until everything is heated through and the rice is slightly crispy.
10. Garnish the fried rice with sliced green onions, if desired.
11. Serve the Tofu Fried Rice hot, and enjoy!

Soft Tofu Kimchi Soup

Soft Tofu Kimchi Soup is a delicious, traditional Korean dish that is both nutritious and easy to make. It is rich in flavor due to the combination of kimchi, vegetables, and seasonings slowly simmered into a savory broth. This soup is satisfying, flavourful, and has many health benefits as it is high in protein and dietary fiber.

Ingredients:

- 2 tablespoons vegetable oil
- 4 cloves garlic, minced
- 1 small onion, chopped
- 2 tablespoons gochujang (Korean red pepper flakes)
- 1/2 cup kimchi, chopped
- 4 cups vegetable or chicken broth
- 1 block of soft tofu, cut into small cubes
- 2 tablespoons soy sauce
- 2 green onions, chopped
- Salt and pepper, to taste
- Optional: 1 egg per serving

Instructions:

1. Heat the vegetable oil in a large pot over medium-high heat.
2. Add the minced garlic and chopped onion, and sauté until the onion is translucent for about 2-3 minutes.

3. Add the gochugaru and stir for about 30 seconds until fragrant.
4. Add the chopped kimchi to the pot and sauté for another 2-3 minutes.
5. Pour the vegetable or chicken broth into the pot and boil.
6. Reduce the heat to medium-low and add the cubed soft tofu to the pot.
7. Add the soy sauce to the pot and stir gently.
8. Simmer the soup for 5-10 minutes until the tofu is heated.
9. Add salt and pepper to taste.
10. If desired, crack an egg into the center of each serving bowl.
11. Ladle the hot soup over the egg and sprinkle with chopped green onions.
12. Serve the Soft Tofu Kimchi Soup hot with rice or other side dishes.

Roasted Tofu With Chili And Salt

Tofu is a versatile and delicious food that can be enjoyed in many dishes. Roasted tofu with chili and salt is an easy yet tasty way to enjoy the flavors of this protein-packed food. This recipe adds heat from the chili powder and a punch of flavor from the salt. It's a simple dish that can be made in under 30 minutes, making it ideal for busy weeknights when you don't have time to spend hours in the kitchen.

Ingredients:

- 1 block of firm tofu
- 1 tablespoon chili powder
- 1 teaspoon sea salt
- 2 tablespoons olive oil
- Lime wedges for serving (optional)

Instructions:

1. Preheat the oven to 400°F (200°C).
2. Cut the tofu into 1-inch cubes.
3. Mix the chili powder, sea salt, and olive oil in a bowl.
4. Add the cubed tofu to the bowl and toss until the tofu is evenly coated with the chili and salt mixture.
5. Spread the tofu cubes out in a single layer on a baking sheet.
6. Roast the tofu in the oven for 20-25 minutes, until it is crispy and lightly browned outside.
7. Serve the Roasted Tofu with Chili and Salt hot, garnished with lime wedges, if desired.

8. This dish makes a great appetizer or snack, or it can be served as a main course alongside vegetables and rice.

Green Curry With Tofu

Green curry is a delicious Thai dish that can be made with many variations. Tofu is an ideal substitute for the traditional proteins used in this recipe for those looking for a vegetarian option. This article will provide an easy-to-follow guide on making a classic green curry with tofu that tastes authentic and packs a flavorful punch. You'll enjoy a delicious meal without compromising taste or texture with just the right combination of spices, vegetables, and tofu.

Ingredients:

- 1 block of firm tofu, cubed
- 1 tablespoon vegetable oil
- 2 tablespoons green curry paste
- 1 can of coconut milk
- 1 red bell pepper, sliced
- 1 green bell pepper, sliced
- 1 small zucchini, sliced
- 1 cup green beans, trimmed
- 1 tablespoon soy sauce
- 1 tablespoon brown sugar
- 1 tablespoon lime juice
- Salt and pepper, to taste
- Fresh cilantro, chopped, for serving
- Cooked rice for serving

Instructions:

1. Heat the vegetable oil in a large pot over medium heat.
2. Add the green curry paste to the pot and stir for about 1-2 minutes until fragrant.
3. Pour in the can of coconut milk and stir to combine.
4. Add the sliced red and green bell peppers, zucchini, and trimmed green beans to the pot.
5. Add the cubed tofu to the pot and stir gently.
6. Add the soy sauce, brown sugar, and lime juice to the pot and stir to combine.
7. Bring the curry to a simmer and cook for 10-15 minutes, occasionally stirring, until the vegetables are tender and the curry has thickened.
8. Season with salt and pepper to taste.
9. Serve the Green Curry with Tofu hot, garnished with chopped cilantro, and alongside cooked rice.
10. This delicious and fragrant curry is a perfect vegetarian main course, packed with flavor and nutrients.

Fried Tofu With Tamarind Sauce

Tofu is an incredibly versatile food that can be cooked and prepared in many different ways. One of the most delicious is fried tofu with tamarind sauce which combines the unique flavor of tamarind with the firm texture of fried tofu. This dish is a delightful way to enjoy tofu and is quick and easy to make.

Ingredients:

- 1 block of firm tofu, drained and cut into cubes
- 1/4 cup cornstarch
- 1/4 cup all-purpose flour
- 1/2 teaspoon salt
- 1/4 teaspoon black pepper
- 2 tablespoons vegetable oil for frying
- 1/4 cup tamarind concentrate
- 1/4 cup water
- 2 tablespoons soy sauce
- 2 tablespoons brown sugar
- 1 tablespoon cornstarch
- 1/4 cup chopped green onions, for garnish

Instructions:

1. Mix the cornstarch, all-purpose flour, salt, and black pepper in a bowl.
2. Dredge the tofu cubes in the flour mixture until they are coated evenly.

3. In a large frying pan, heat the vegetable oil over medium-high heat.
4. Fry the coated tofu cubes in the hot oil until they are golden brown and crispy on all sides, about 4-5 minutes.
5. Remove the tofu from the pan and place it on a paper towel to drain any excess oil.
6. Mix the tamarind concentrate, water, soy sauce, brown sugar, and cornstarch in a small saucepan until smooth.
7. Cook the tamarind sauce over medium heat, stirring constantly, until it thickens and becomes glossy, about 2-3 minutes.
8. Drizzle the tamarind sauce over the fried tofu cubes.
9. Garnish with chopped green onions.
10. Serve the Fried Tofu with Tamarind Sauce hot as an appetizer or side dish.
11. This dish is a delicious blend of crispy tofu and sweet and tangy tamarind sauce.

Tofu And Pork Hamburger

Tofu and pork hamburger is a unique and delicious food combination that vegans and meat lovers can enjoy! This dish brings together two of the most popular proteins, tofu and pork, to create an exciting meal that is sure to please. With the perfect balance of texture and flavor, this burger bursts with plant-based protein and a variety of vegetables for added nutrition.

Ingredients:

- 1 block firm tofu, drained and crumbled
- 1/2 pound ground pork
- 1/2 cup breadcrumbs
- 1 egg
- 1 tablespoon soy sauce
- 1 teaspoon sesame oil
- 1 teaspoon ginger, minced
- 1 teaspoon garlic, minced
- Salt and pepper, to taste
- 4 hamburger buns
- Lettuce leaves, tomato slices, and sliced onions for serving

Instructions:

1. In a mixing bowl, combine the crumbled tofu, ground pork, breadcrumbs, egg, soy sauce, sesame oil, ginger, garlic, salt, and pepper. Mix well.

2. Divide the mixture into four portions and shape each part into a patty.
3. Heat a large skillet over medium heat.
4. Add the patties to the skillet and cook for about 5-6 minutes on each side until they are cooked through and golden brown.
5. Toast the hamburger buns and assemble the hamburgers with lettuce leaves, tomato slices, and sliced onions.
6. Serve the Tofu and Pork Hamburger hot, and enjoy!
7. This recipe is a unique twist on a classic hamburger, with the addition of tofu for extra protein and texture.

Spinach Tofu Cutlets

Spinach Tofu Cutlets are the perfect choice if you're looking for an easy and delicious vegan meal. This simple recipe is full of flavor and healthy ingredients that everyone in the family can enjoy. Made with tofu, spinach, onion, garlic, and spices, these cutlets make a great alternative to a traditional meat-based dish. Plus, they can be served as a main course or as a side dish to accompany any vegan meal.

Ingredients:

- 1 block of firm tofu, drained and mashed
- 1 cup fresh spinach, finely chopped
- 1/2 cup breadcrumbs
- 1/2 cup all-purpose flour
- 1 egg
- 1 tablespoon soy sauce
- 1/2 teaspoon garlic powder
- 1/4 teaspoon black pepper
- Salt, to taste
- 2-3 tablespoons vegetable oil

Instructions:

1. Mix the mashed tofu, finely chopped spinach, breadcrumbs, all-purpose flour, egg, soy sauce, garlic powder, black pepper, and salt in a mixing bowl. Mix well.
2. Shape the mixture into small cutlets or patties.

3. Heat the vegetable oil in a large frying pan over medium heat.
4. Add the cutlets to the pan and cook for about 4-5 minutes on each side until they are golden brown and crispy.
5. Remove the cutlets from the pan and place them on a paper towel to drain any excess oil.
6. Serve the Spinach Tofu Cutlets hot with steamed vegetables, rice, or salad.
7. These cutlets are a healthy and delicious way to enjoy tofu and spinach, and they make a great vegetarian main course or appetizer.

Tofu Steamed Egg

Tofu steamed egg is a delicious and healthy dish that's easy to make. This simple Asian-style dish combines soft, silken tofu with eggs for a savory meal suitable for any time of day. Not only does it taste great, but it also contains some nutritional benefits that make it an ideal choice for those looking to include more plant-based proteins in their diet.

Ingredients:

- 1 block of soft tofu, drained and cut into cubes
- 3 large eggs
- 1 1/2 cups chicken or vegetable broth
- 1 tablespoon soy sauce
- 1 teaspoon sesame oil
- 1/2 teaspoon salt
- 1/4 teaspoon white pepper
- Green onions, chopped, for garnish

Instructions:

1. In a mixing bowl, whisk the eggs until they are well beaten.
2. Add the chicken or vegetable broth, soy sauce, sesame oil, salt, and white pepper. Mix well.
3. Pour the egg mixture into a heatproof dish.
4. Arrange the tofu cubes on top of the egg mixture.
5. Fill a steamer pot with water and bring it to a boil.
6. Place the heatproof dish into the steamer and steam the Tofu Steamed Egg for 15-20 minutes until the egg is set.

7. Garnish with chopped green onions and serve hot.
8. This dish is a comforting and healthy way to enjoy tofu and eggs, and it makes a great breakfast, lunch, or dinner.

Tofu Tomato Sauce Pasta

Tofu Tomato Sauce Pasta is an easy, tasty, and healthy meal that can be prepared in less than 30 minutes. Not only is it a great vegan alternative to traditional pasta dishes, but it is also a fantastic source of protein and vitamins. In addition, the combination of tofu and tomato sauce makes for a delicious and savory dish that will please anyone's palate.

Ingredients:

- 1 block of firm tofu, drained and crumbled
- 1 pound pasta, any kind
- 1 can of crushed tomatoes
- 1 small onion, chopped
- 4 cloves garlic, minced
- 2 tablespoons olive oil
- 1 tablespoon tomato paste
- 1/2 teaspoon dried oregano
- 1/2 teaspoon dried basil
- 1/4 teaspoon red pepper flakes
- Salt and pepper, to taste
- Parmesan cheese, grated, for serving (optional)

Instructions:

1. Cook the pasta according to the package instructions until it is al dente. Drain and set aside.
2. In a large saucepan, heat the olive oil over medium heat.

3. Add the chopped onion and minced garlic to the saucepan and sauté for about 2-3 minutes until the onion is translucent.
4. Add the crumbled tofu to the saucepan and sauté for 3-4 minutes until the tofu is lightly browned.
5. Add the crushed tomatoes, tomato paste, oregano, dried basil, red pepper flakes, salt, and pepper to the saucepan.
6. Stir well and bring the sauce to a simmer.
7. Simmer the sauce for 10-15 minutes, occasionally stirring, until it has thickened.
8. Add the cooked pasta to the saucepan and toss until it is evenly coated with the tomato sauce.
9. Serve the Tofu Tomato Sauce Pasta hot, garnished with grated Parmesan cheese, if desired.
10. This dish is a healthy and flavorful way to enjoy tofu and pasta, making it a great vegetarian main course.

Baked Tofu With Vermicelli

Are you looking for a hearty but healthy meal that can be prepared quickly and easily? Look no further than baked tofu with vermicelli! This simple yet delicious dish is packed with protein, fiber, vitamins, and minerals to ensure you get all the energy and nourishment you need. The best part of this meal is that it takes minimal effort to prepare; all you have to do is mix some ingredients and bake in the oven.

Ingredients:

- 1 block of firm tofu, drained and cut into cubes
- 4 oz vermicelli noodles
- 1 red bell pepper, sliced
- 1 small onion, sliced
- 1 tablespoon vegetable oil
- 1 tablespoon soy sauce
- 1 tablespoon brown sugar
- 1 tablespoon rice vinegar
- 1 tablespoon cornstarch
- 1/4 cup water
- 1/4 cup chopped green onions
- Salt and pepper, to taste

Instructions:

1. Preheat the oven to 375°F (190°C).
2. Arrange the tofu cubes on a baking sheet lined with parchment paper.

3. Bake the tofu in the oven for 15-20 minutes until it is lightly browned and crispy.
4. While the tofu is baking, cook the vermicelli noodles according to the package instructions.
5. Heat the vegetable oil in a large skillet over medium-high heat.
6. Add the sliced red bell pepper and onion to the skillet and sauté for about 2-3 minutes until the vegetables are tender.
7. Whisk together the soy sauce, brown sugar, rice vinegar, cornstarch, water, salt, and pepper in a mixing bowl.
8. Pour the sauce mixture into the skillet with the vegetables and stir to combine.
9. Add the cooked vermicelli noodles to the skillet and toss until they are evenly coated with the sauce.
10. Add the baked tofu cubes to the skillet and toss gently to combine.
11. Simmer the mixture for 2-3 minutes until the sauce has thickened.
12. Remove the skillet from the heat and garnish with chopped green onions.
13. Serve the Baked Tofu with Vermicelli hot, and enjoy!
14. This dish is a healthy and flavorful way to enjoy tofu and vermicelli noodles, making it a great vegetarian main course.

Spinach Pesto With Tofu

Are you looking for a delicious and easy way to add extra nutrition to your meals? Look no further than spinach pesto with tofu! This recipe is quick and straightforward to make yet incredibly flavorful. It is packed with essential vitamins and minerals and can also be enjoyed as a snack or part of any meal. You can whip up this vegan-friendly dish using just a few ingredients and spices in minutes.

Ingredients:

- 1 block of firm tofu, drained and cut into cubes
- 2 cups fresh spinach, washed and dried
- 1/2 cup fresh basil leaves
- 1/4 cup grated Parmesan cheese
- 1/4 cup pine nuts or walnuts
- 3 cloves garlic, minced
- 1/4 cup olive oil
- Salt and pepper, to taste
- Cooked pasta for serving

Instructions:

1. Bring salted water to a boil in a large pot and cook the pasta according to the package instructions until it is al dente. Drain and set aside.
2. Combine the fresh spinach, fresh basil leaves, grated Parmesan cheese, pine nuts or walnuts, and minced garlic in a blender or food processor. Pulse until the mixture is finely chopped.

3. While the blender or food processor is running, slowly pour in the olive oil until the mixture is smooth and well blended.
4. Season the spinach pesto with salt and pepper to taste.
5. In a large skillet, sauté the cubed tofu over medium-high heat until it is golden brown on all sides.
6. Add the spinach pesto to the skillet with the tofu and stir until the tofu is coated evenly with the pesto.
7. Serve the Spinach Pesto with hot tofu, over cooked pasta.
8. This dish is a healthy and delicious way to enjoy tofu and spinach pesto, and it makes a great vegetarian main course.

Tofu Meatballs

Tofu meatballs are an incredibly versatile and delicious alternative to traditional meat-based recipes. Perfect for vegetarians, vegans, or anyone looking to add plant-based proteins to their meals, tofu meatballs are easy to make and require only a few simple ingredients. They can be enjoyed on their own as a tasty dish or used to jazz up pizza, sandwiches, or salads.

Ingredients:

- 1 block of firm tofu, drained and crumbled
- 1/2 cup breadcrumbs
- 1/2 cup grated Parmesan cheese
- 1/4 cup chopped fresh parsley
- 2 cloves garlic, minced
- 1 egg
- 1 tablespoon soy sauce
- 1 tablespoon olive oil
- Salt and pepper, to taste

Instructions:

1. Preheat the oven to 375°F (190°C).
2. In a mixing bowl, combine the crumbled tofu, breadcrumbs, grated Parmesan cheese, chopped fresh parsley, minced garlic, egg, soy sauce, olive oil, salt, and pepper. Mix well.

3. Roll the mixture into small meatball shapes, about 1 inch in diameter.
4. Place the meatballs on a baking sheet lined with parchment paper.
5. Bake the Tofu Meatballs in the oven for 15-20 minutes until they are golden brown and crispy.
6. Remove the Tofu Meatballs from the oven and serve hot with your favorite dipping sauce, or toss with your favorite pasta sauce and cooked pasta.
7. These meatballs are a healthy and delicious way to enjoy tofu and make a great vegetarian appetizer, main course, or snack.

Made in United States
North Haven, CT
31 May 2024